Introspection: A Collection Of Poetry

Amanda Trent

BookLeaf
Publishing

Presentation by *BookLeaf Publishing*

Web: www.bookleafpub.com

E-mail: info@bookleafpub.com

ISBN: 9789357612753

First edition 2022

PREFACE

We are resilient
And tough, ever growing
And branching out,
Protecting others from the rain,
like trees.
But, also like trees,
In order to survive,
we still need to be watered.

Quick Sand

Cartoons always depicted quick sand,
So I assumed it'd be a common threat.
But as I aged, I realized
I had no real need to fret.

Because I haven't seen any quick sand,
At least, not in the physical sense.
What I thought was a looming danger,
Has only left me in suspense.

But it doesn't look like I thought,
It lies, disguised, ready to attack.
I fell in before I saw it, and
It snared me before I could turn back.

It just looked like a normal patch of life.
Yet here I am, sinking and screaming.
I'm order to get out of this mess,
I'll grab and hold on to anything.

Anyone, help me, please,
I'm desperate as I descend.
Anything, please, anything,
Just make this shame end.

Twister

Sad thoughts are hard to carry,
They can be heavy, and even scary.
Depression, guilt, and shame,
All lead to self-hatred and blame.
A downward spiral, too hard to escape,
Full of insults that bump and scrape.
The thoughts lead one to weep,
Weeping leads one to sleep.
The sleep leads to indolence,
Indolence to self-offense.
A cry for help is pushed aside,
For no one cares why I've cried.
I got swept up and carried away.
Pull me out of my own head, I pray.

Dreamer

I dream of the world.
I hold it in my hands and leap
Towards my ambitions as I sleep.
The world one day will be mine,
Everything by my design.

But I miss the jump and hit a bump.

I dream of serenity.
Not quite happy, but at peace,
With an ironed life that has a crease.
It isn't perfect, a tad confused,
A tasteless peach, a little bruised.

But I smack into a wall and fall.

I have a nightmare about driving my car.
I just sit and stare at a tree
That stands so tall in front of little me.
One swift move and it can all go away.
Yet, Somehow, I still stand today.

Socially Anxious

You say I'm quiet, uptight, and shy.
But my mind goes empty, void, and dry.

My arms break out, and my head aches,
My jaw clamps shut and my body shakes.

People aren't always gawking,
That's just the anxiety talking.

I know I'm not likable, easy to overlook.
But with a little more time, my latch will
unhook.

I may seem boring, but please understand,
I promise there's more to the bland.

"Don't say the wrong thing, don't overshare".
Why is it me that's under your stare?

I want to talk and do so with ease,
But how do I do so when I only displease?

Just to chat takes so much work.
And still, "you're so quiet, such a quirk."

I hate myself for being this way,
But what do I do, what do I say?
                    5

That's the question, always on my mind.
The kindness is there, it's words I can't find.

This Side of My Skin

On the outside, I am calm and collected.
On the inside, I am disconnected.

On the outside, I am soft and quiet.
On the inside, my mind is in a riot.

On the outside, I seem able and smart.
On the inside, I can't hear through my thumping
heart.

On the outside, my eyes appear bright and clear.
On the inside, I'm plagued with fear.

On the outside, I am hard to read.
On the inside, my head and heart have disagreed

On the outside, I appear indifferent.
On the inside, everything is an irritant.

On the outside, I remain a mystery.
On the inside, my mind is misery.

On the outside, I act submissive.
On the inside, I am captive.

Silhouette

I scream and flail about,
Drowning in tears as I shout
Your name, time after time.
My existence feels like a crime.
What are you even looking toward
To leave me here, alone and ignored.
Maybe I should just disappear,
Since you already pretend I'm not here.
From just being me, I'm swathed in shame,
For no matter how loud I scream your name,
thrash about, writhe and fret,
All I see is your silhouette.

She Could Have Been So Much More

She keeps quiet
For all the times she was ignored.
What's the point of talking
If no one is listening?

She keeps quiet,
For all the times she was laughed at.
Why share her ideas
When no one thinks she's good enough?

She keeps quiet,
For all the times she was questioned.
Why trust herself
When no one else does?

She keeps quiet
For all the times she was forgotten.
Why even try
When she isn't worth it?

All The Versions I Was Before

In my childhood bedroom, I've left myself at the door.
Instead, I become all the versions I was before.

The child who dreamed on a cloud of stuffed animals.
Full of wonder and potential, the cynicism minimal.

The games that were played here, the possibilities explored.
A child, nothing and everything. An exciting journey, I moved toward.

A tired, optimistic teenager, still searching for my purpose.
Trying on different versions, that may not reach beneath the surface.

Years searching for answers: Where will I go? Who will I be?
The adults said, "Anywhere and anything! You are free!"

Until reality gave a different answer: "How
much do you possess?
Money, talent, confidence, to be anyone worthy,
you must have excess."

But for a while, I can pretend that I did not just
lay down and concede.
I stand beside my childhood bed as the version
still full of hope and dreams.

A Letter

I was told that in order to heal,
I should write a letter to my abuser.
But if I deserved the torture,
Am I a victim or an accuser?

Your words cut deep into my soul,
Where they scarred and maimed.
You put me in a cycle of self hatred,
And for that you should be ashamed.

But, I know that you already are,
There's nothing you feel more.
But don't forget to feel regret
That I'm more damaged than before.

For years on end, I hated you.
And that hatred will be forever.
It will worm its way through
Every thought and endeavor.

This letter really didn't help at all.
It didn't make anything clearer.
But I guess that should be expected
When the recipient is in the mirror.

Who Am I Without You?

When I take the "you" out of me, who am I?
What kind of soul will remain?
When you carefully crafted every piece,
Will it still linger, the damage or pain?

When I am of your making,
How do I become my own person?
I liked who I was when I was by your side,
But now I see another version.

A better version, I must say.
I thought you were a saint.
But now I see you were a parasite,
A bully and a constraint.

I see the world so differently now,
In a much sweeter, brighter hue.
I thought I was safe in your embrace,
But I shall now make my debut.

A new me, a kinder me,
A hopeful dreamer restored.
I now realize what you killed inside,
Before it could be explored.

When I take the "you" out of me, who am I?
I'm no longer just a myth.
I'm a stronger, more vibrant being,
A force to be reckoned with.

Colors

The yellow sun shone bright as I stood upright.
Upon my face, I wore a grin, and lifted my chin.
Life was worthwhile, and I could smile.
Always looking upward and forward.

But the clouds cried blue, the darkness a clue,
Down came sad tears from wasted years.
Regret and shame, the ones to blame.
Trapped underwater, a disappointing daughter.

The fire burned red, because I'd made my bed,
And lay in it I must, despite the disgust.
The anger eats away, and I continue to betray
Myself and my goals, my future now full of
holes.

The sky is still gray, closing my airway.
Done, forgotten, my dark soul rotten.
Hope said "bye," now I just comply,
Dejected and dull, not sad, nor mad.

But I'm still here, between the green
Grass and trees, among the bees.
Spring has sprung, and I've begun
Removing the thorns and grabbing the horns.

My Own Worst Enemy

Always in search of answers,
To my own woe and misery,
I let the days pass by me,
Considering every theory.

I compare myself to others,
Wanting what they possess,
I now recognize that I'm the one
Keeping myself from success.

To my own disappointment,
I overthink and worry too much.
For reasons, even I don't understand,
I use my anxiety as a crutch.

But confessing that is the first step,
To moving on with my life.
Now I can finally heal,
Since I know who's holding the knife.

Moving on and forward,
I won't remain stuck here in my ways.
I'm thinking more simply,
And looking towards brighter days.

Ups and Downs

The leaves rustle with the wind,
Among the trees I find a friend,
Against the worry they defend,
And I no longer need to pretend.

But again the darkness finds me,
From the dread I won't be free,
Certainty and promise flee,
My fight or flight cannot agree.

And then the canaries sing,
A melody in revival spring,
A dose of solace upon their wing,
And to the comfort I will cling.

Disdain and fear once more descend,
A clever hunter I must commend,
Sorrow I just pray will end,
To the darkness, I fall and blend.

Yet, the sun's warmth thaws the freeze,
A mellow consolation breeze,
Someone, somewhere heard my pleas,
And I gravitate towards ease.

Let Go and Move On

Let go and move on,
That's how the story goes.
There has been no closure,
Yet, it still comes to a close.

But how does one forget
The apology that will never come.
The lingering doubt of worth,
To which I succumb.

How does one go as normal,
While you're out there spinning lies.
I shouldn't take your insults,
Since I'd never ask for your advice.

Reality makes you look bad,
So you disregard and twist it.
With exaggerations floating about,
How shall I forget?

I shall never tell my side,
What would be the use?
Speaking my story out loud
only tightens the noose.

Just a Mom

Besides the tears, upon my face, I feel a tiny palm,
I go by many names, my favorite of them is,
"Mom".

I try to hold it in, I try not to let them see,
The desperation and insecurities that consume me.

Because I am a person, a real human being.
I'm a breathing, feeling woman, not a robot, nor a thing.

My skin is real skin, it's not made of steel.
But I am not allowed to feel what I feel.

I try to do things right, but somehow still screw up.
But I can only pour so much from a half empty cup.

If I go to work or stay at home, either way is wrong.
Everywhere, anytime, is where I belong.

For anything and everything, I will be shamed.
For anything and everything, I'm to be blamed.

"You do not deserve a break, don't you dare
complain a word,"
But even robots need to recharge, so that you
can be served.

It's not the kids that are wearing me down, it's
you that's pissing me off,
For every move I make, you disapprove and
scoff.

"Just shut up, cook dinner, do some laundry,
wash the dishes!"
My whole existence is to serve, no matter what
my wishes.

I will gladly serve the kids, with a smile on my
face.
But you also demand my hand and tell me to
learn my place.

Because I have no other worth, no real purpose,
Except for maintaining this three ring circus.

It's a pretty big job, the most desired and most
rejected,

For I am just a Mom, trying to do everything
that is expected.

What Did You Do All Day?

If a mom wants a cup of coffee,
She'll have to make it herself.
As she's pouring the water,
She'll see an empty cup on the shelf.

It will remind her that the kids need a drink,
So she'll look for their sippy cups.
While searching, she'll begin
Picking the toys and tiny socks up.

Which will remind her of the
Laundry she forgot to start.
She'll notice the laundry soap is low,
So she'll go to add it to her cart.

When she grabs her phone,
She'll see a reminder, "light bill due."
While paying the bill, a kid will bring her
A book they want read through.

So she'll read the book,
And smell something gross.
She'll change their diaper,
And notice lunch time is close.

She'll finally have a moment
To wash the dishes while the kids eat.
But she'll hear, "I have to go potty,"
So she'll help them up to the seat.

When she washes her hands,
She'll notice the hand towel on the floor.
She'll dry her hands with a paper towel,
But the trash is still full from the day before.

She'll pull the bag out, but it might rip,
Spilling the trash all about.
So she'll pick it all up,
Filling the trash she just tried to take out.

While trying to keep the kids out of the mess,
She'll give them a snack of goldfish.
But while she sweeps and mops up the trash,
The kids might dump their dish.

So she'll have to vacuum,
But she should probably dust first.
While dusting, she'll find a sippy cup
And remember the kids' thirst.

So she'll fill it up and feel her head
Throb from no caffeine.
So she'll try again to make her coffee,

And put the kids in front of the screen.

As the coffee is brewing,
She'll feel guilt and shame.
So she'll leave her coffee, turn off the TV
And sit down to play a game.

When she hears her husband pull in,
Expecting the house to be clean,
She'll rush all around
To quickly tidy the scene.

And she'll feel even more of that guilt
And shame, and even anxiety.
Because she isn't perfect
Like other moms in society.

Then her husband will come in,
Look around, and say,
"What did you even do all day?"

I Am Trying

I am done using my anxiety as a crutch.

Alive and happy, full of purpose,
More worth, and less worthless.

Trying to keep my eyes open wide.
Ready to look on the bright side.
Yearning to feel pride.
I will no longer be a pretender.
Never willing to surrender,
Going on a new adventure.

Control

25

I always look down when I walk
for I don't trust the ground to always be there.
I keep my eyes on the ground,
So I can account for a hole anywhere.

I organize and calculate,
I don't do spontaneity well.
For if you do not have an outline,
How will you excel?

But if you want to make God laugh,
Tell him of your plans and goals.
For when things don't go as you thought,
You'll soon learn who is in control.

Draft

I hope to never fully learn my craft,
And to always remain a draft,

Because to mark every book as "read,"
To be unwavering in every word said,

To hold all the knowledge in my mind,
To discover every treasure there is to find,

To greet every face there is to meet,
To travel down every street,

To complete each possible quest,
To succeed in every test,

To accomplish every goal,
To identify as completely whole,

To master every skill there is to know,
Means there is nowhere else to go.

But I Can

I cannot sing with substantial range,
But I can forgive and turn the page.

I cannot dance with sophisticated motion,
But I can feel deeply every emotion.

I cannot play an instrument with any virtuosity,
But I can show kindness and generosity.

I cannot use any dexterity to paint,
But I can withhold a futile complaint.

I cannot recall formulas from memory,
But I can show patience and empathy.

Sometimes, God keeps our skills undecorated,
But even the littlest sparrow is celebrated.

All the Proof I Need

You ask why I believe in the word
Of a voice that cannot be heard.
Or follow someone I can't see,
Whose presence I can't guarantee.

Why, if I can't even feel His hand?
If you have to ask, you won't understand.
Because I CAN hear, see, and feel,
And I'll never deny that He is real.

I hear Him in the sermons that come at just the right time.
Like at the moment when I'm standing at the line,
Between barely functioning and ghost.
But then I hear, "He loves you" when I needed to the most.

I see His blessings in the eyes of my boys,
Through all the nighttime wakings, diaper changes, and noise.
A surprise I didn't know I needed,
A saving grace for which I pleaded.

I feel His presence as I lay awake at night,

Worrying about money, and doing what's right.
A calmness comes over me, from a gentle palm.
I may not feel the hand, but I can feel the calm.

www.ingramcontent.com/pod-product-compliance
Lightning Source LLC
Chambersburg PA
CBHW070726160726
48003CB00006BA/2394